Learn to
CATCH WITH KATY
and friends!

As a primary school teacher and having played sport at both a professional and international level, I can say with confidence that being able to catch gives a child so many more opportunities in the playground and on the sports field. Possessing the ability to catch leads to inclusion, confidence and ultimately to happiness.

To catch is to see, predict, move, balance, judge, time and grasp.

for Hollie, Daisy & Bella

and Daisy & Bea

Hello!

I'm Katy! In this book, my friends and I will show you lots of fun ways to learn to catch. Let's get started!

Katy hits it
nice and high...

watch her keep
it in the sky.

This time as it's falling down...

can she wrap her arms around?

Roll the ball, it's fun to do...

forwards, backwards, me to you.

Try it lying on your tummy...

just like Charlie and his Mummy.

Now it's time to find a winner,
a game or two before your dinner.

Roll it left and roll it right,
stop the ball with all your might.

Now for throwing...
up it goes!

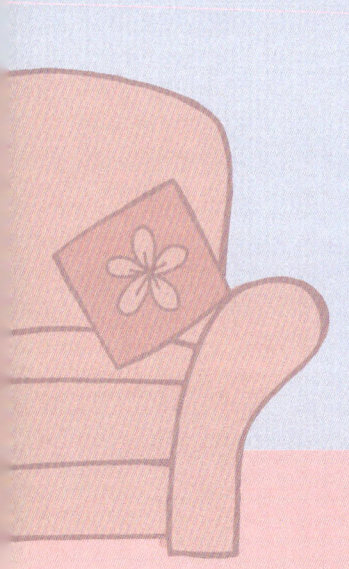

Start quite low,
keep on your toes.

Daisy tried it sitting, kneeling.

Reggie caught it, what a feeling!

Competition time again,
can you make it up to ten?

Me to you and you to me.
Watch, focus, ready? One, two, three.

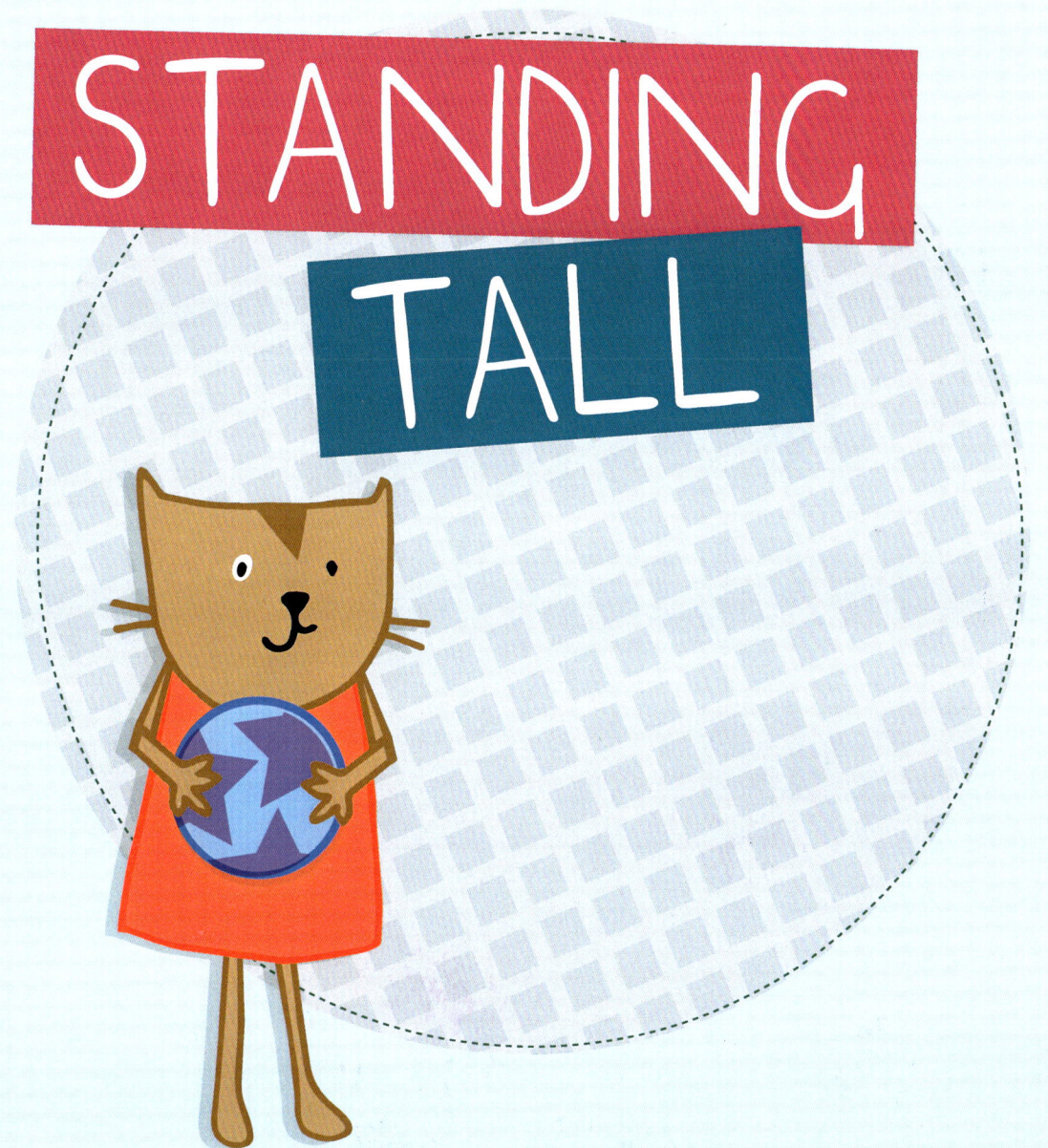

Bella stands now, knees bent, steady...

Katy throws... are Bella's arms out ready?

Watch the ball and then you'll catch it.

Well done Bella, that's fantastic!

High throw, low throw, left and right;
practise morning, noon and night.

To make it harder, just use hands.
Can you clap before it lands?

Hollie plays with a smaller ball...

she bounces, catches down the hall.

Miss it, spill it, fumble, drop.

Try again Hollie, never stop!

20

A new best friend is here to stay, anytime is good for play!

Two hands, one hand, against a wall.
Can you spin then catch the ball?

You've done so well.

You've passed the test.

One more thing before it ends...

PARENTS' TIPS

BALLOON FUN

- **Encourage** your child to hit both under and overarm.
- Look for your child to be light on their feet (small steps).
- Can the balloon be caught with hands only?

ROLL-A-BALL

- **Praise** your child for keeping their eyes on the ball.
- Focus more on them stopping the ball rather than rolling.
- Set up two goals and try to score - make it **fun**!

CUSHION CATCH

- Don't throw too high, you could drop from above.
- Use body & arms to clamp around cushion - **reward** all success.
- Always model the catch for your child - remember to fix your eyes on the cushion.

STANDING TALL

- Use a beach ball or softer plastic ball.
- Let ball hit chest and wrap arms around.
- **Encourage** soft hands and elbows when catching hands only.

YOU, ME AND BALL

- The more your child plays with balls of all sizes, the more comfortable and **confident** they will become.
- So much **fun**, in such a simple way!

SMALL BALL

- Start with low compression tennis balls.
- Allow your child to play in the house - have a ball with them at all times.
- Your child will learn how a ball reacts in flight and after bouncing.
- Keep setting **challenges**.

Learn to Catch with Katy and friends! First published by Steven Perkins 2016
This edition published 2016
Text © Steven Perkins 2016
Illustrations © Holly Newth 2016

The moral rights of the author and the illustrator have been asserted.
All rights reserved.
No part of this publication may be reproduced, stored in a retrieval system
or transmitted in any form or by any means, electrical, mechanical,
photocopying, recording or otherwise, without prior permission
of the author and the illustrator. Any person who does
an unauthorised act in relation to this publication may be
liable to criminal prosecution and civil claims for damages.

Printed by Printondemand-worldwide
ISBN 978-0-9935627-1-6

www.katycatch.com